MW01287512

APPLAUSE
FOR
A CLOUD

Applause for a Cloud

雲へ拍手

by Sayumi Kamakura

Translated by James Shea

Black Ocean
Boston · Chicago

To reprint, reproduce, or transmit electronically, or by recording all or part of this manuscript, beyond brief reviews or educational purposes, please send a written request to the publisher at:

Black Ocean
P.O. Box 52030
Boston, MA 02205
blackocean.org

Cover and Book Design by Janaka Stucky | janakastucky.com

ISBN: 978-1-939568-99-1

Library of Congress Control Number: 2025931510

Printed in Canada

FIRST EDITION

CONTENTS

Translator's Note

On a recent trip to Japan, I walked into Kinokuniya, one of the country's largest and oldest bookstore chains. Set off from the shelves labeled "poetry," I found two bookcases dedicated to haiku and tanka. They included anthologies, essay collections, handbooks, and single-authored collections, all related to contemporary and modern haiku and tanka. It was a reminder of how these forms retain a special place in Japanese letters—they are poetry, but also exist somewhat outside of poetry, as if they were distinct genres. In Japan, and elsewhere, writing haiku is more than a poetic form; it is a kind of devotion. Many haiku poets, such as Sayumi Kamakura, write only haiku.

At 72, Kamakura is one of Japan's leading haiku poets. She began writing while still a student at Saitama University in the 1970s; in addition to her major work, *The Collected Haiku of Sayumi Kamakura* (*Kamakura Sayumi Zenkushū*), she has now authored more than ten volumes of haiku along with various essays. Her writing has appeared in dozens of anthologies in Japan and overseas, and she is the only haiku poet featured in *Japanese Women Poets: An Anthology*, edited by Hiroaki Sato. Kamakura's awards include the Oki Sango Prize and the Modern Haiku Association Prize.

When I asked her about the difference between writing haiku and writing poetry, Kamakura said they both entail the expression of one's inner self. But because haiku is short and needs to omit so many elements, it requires an ability to decide what to remove and what to keep ("it's a calculation of words"). Although such economy of language is difficult, it's also where the appeal of haiku lies for Kamakura. At the same time, many of her haiku do not follow the form's traditional requirements, such as the strict use of seventeen syllables and a seasonal word. Her work resists narrow definitions of the form that persist today, in favor of a more expansive and challenging framework. I have been translating Kamakura's haiku for the past twenty years, and I worked closely with her on these translations, often asking about the nuances of a particular word or the meaning of an entire poem, to ensure that I understood as much as possible—especially when such brief works permit so many interpretations: in general, Japanese haiku omit pronouns, do not distinguish between singular and plural nouns, and allow more syntactic flexibility than English poetry.

The wide range of moods and valences in Kamakura's haiku feels diaristic, as if tracking subtle changes in her emotional life. Her poems can be simultaneously wise, funny, gentle, and shocking: suddenly winter has a bone, spring becomes an object in one's pocket, and summer passes through the hole of a donut. The brevity of the form makes her haiku impossible to argue with—you either buy it or you don't. Her conceits are usually drawn from everyday life, even though occasionally she alludes to legends from world literature and Japanese mythological figures, especially female deities. Kamakura brings a cosmological perspective to bear on daily life, setting our corporeality in relief against the universe. Her imagery moves effortlessly and tenderly between the majestic and the banal, the macro and the micro, often with a tone that welcomes humor or a beginner's mind.

Another Kamakura hallmark is her frequent use of personification, a feature more prevalent in her work than in other contemporary or even classical haiku poets. Kamakura has said she likes the way anthropomorphism opens her imagination and allows for haiku that are not focused solely on reality. Comparing Kamakura's haiku to dreamlike fairy tales in which objects and the natural world come to life, the Hungarian literary critic Judit Vihar has also noted Kamakura's penchant for personification. In her preface to *Seven Sunsets* (2013), Vihar writes that in Kamakura's work "humans, things, and nature do not have separate lives."

Even John Ruskin, who coined the term "pathetic fallacy"—to describe a flight by poets who are "borne away, or over-clouded, or over-dazzled by emotion"—recognized that personification can be found in the greatest poets, including Homer. In Kamakura, there's more complexity in the imagery than it may at first seem: due to the general lack of pronouns, for instance, it can be unclear who or what is having the emotional experience. While it could be the speaker, in some cases, it could be the natural phenomenon, or perhaps both at once. Her work evokes Japanese animism, in which it's believed that within every object resides a little god or divine spirit (*kami*). Ruskin in *Modern Painters* (1843–60) observed that the Greeks gave human qualities to the natural world because they believed that the gods were everywhere, and so they could say: "'The tree *is* glad . . . I know it is; I can cut it down: no matter, there was a nymph in it. The water *does* sing . . . I can dry it up; but no matter, there was a naiad in it.'" That a contemporary poet can dedicate her life to rendering the world so rich in sentience feels radical to me. It's hard to describe this vocation as anything other than a form of love.

光

Light

座ること風はレンゲに教わりぬ

もう少し歩けば春月まんまるに

パンジーに水やるついでに小石にも

I water a pansy,
giving some
to a stone as well

If I walk a bit more,
the spring moon
becomes perfectly round

The wind learned
how to sit
from the lotus flowers

春昼の白髪三本あとは数えぬ

暖かくなろう釘が針をさそった

花満開わたしをほったらかしにして

14

Cherry blossoms
in full bloom,
just leave me alone

It's getting warmer—
a nail
provokes a needle

In the spring afternoon,
I count three white hairs—
I won't count anymore

霞むかなティラノサウルスも夫も

牛糞のこころが春の終りかと

鳴くひばり空のこともっと知りたい

The skylark cries out,
wanting to know
the sky a bit better

The cow shit
around here may be
the end of spring

Not sure in this mist—
a tyrannosaurus
or my husband

紅ばらの尖るのは棘だけにおし

木のてっぺんぺんぽん夏が待ち遠しい

心まで濡らさぬほどに若葉雨

Not wet until they're
soaked to the heart—
young leaves in rain

The top of the top
of the tree—
can't wait for summer

Only to a splinter
is the sharpness
of the red rose sharp

水は水を続けよもっと澄むために

団栗に乗ってかすかに空も落ちた

やあ五月くちびるから青空まで

Hi, May—
from my lips
to a blue sky

On a falling acorn
the sky, too,
fell slightly

Water,
continue as water,
make yourself clearer

氷りおり水の嘆きもほほえみも

蓮根の穴です数えてみませんか

憧れもかじかむらしい午前四時

My admiration
seems to numb, too,
at 4 AM

Those are holes
in the lotus root—
why don't you count them?

In frozen ice:
water grieving
and smiling

きさらぎも今日は二十日の雲ひとつ

星を入れ損ねた氷柱からしずく

沈黙は天のやさしさ雪ふるふる

Silence is heaven's
gentleness—
snow falling and falling

An icicle failed
to put a star inside itself—
now it's dripping

February, The Month
of Wearing Extra Clothes—
today's a single cloud on the 20th

草薙の剣は消えて草萌える

わかってる？お尻がスミレ踏んだこと

スイートピー風は君から吹いてくる

Sweet pea flower—
the wind blows
away from you

Do you realize?
You just sat
on a violet

The Kusanagi sword
has disappeared
and grass is sprouting

赤おにの涙もながれ春の川

山越えて春来る　山はいつ来るや

芝ざくら子犬のままでいさせてよ

The moss phlox—
let me stay
as a puppy

Spring arrives
over the mountain

When does the mountain arrive?

A spring river
flows with the tears
of a red ogre

ひとり咲いて二人で揺れるチューリップ

朧からおぼろへ靴の先とがる

まつ毛ふと空に呼ばれぬ花のころ

In the time of cherry blossoms,
eyelashes are suddenly
called toward the sky

From a vague evening
into a hazy night,
the tips of my shoes narrow

A tulip blooms alone
and trembles when
held by two people

どうしてもこちらに来るのね蟻の列

夏の水喉をとおったのは確か

とぼとぼと去りゆく春は見ぬことに

I don't look
at the spring lumbering along
as it passes

Summer water—
it definitely went
down my throat

By all means,
come my way—
a row of ants

夏はあそぶ重たい岩は海にあずけて

肩ぽんと叩く夕焼けではないか

守秘義務など元よりなくて草茂る

There's no such thing
as confidentiality here—
the grass grows rampantly

My shoulder struck
with a slap—isn't it
the glow of a sunset?

A playful summer—
leave those heavy rocks
with the ocean

われの瞳へ吹く薫風を信じたし

さよならの「ら」がブナの樹にもたれていた

ガーゴイル、パリのきれいな雨を語れ

Gargoyles
talking about the clear rain
in Paris

The *ra* of *sayonara*
leaned on a
beech tree

I want to believe
in the summer breeze
blowing into my eyes

緑の夜とおくでガラスの馬いななく

その鴉いい加減に鳴くのをおよし

麦の秋「お早う」から「今晩は」まで

Harvesting wheat
from *Good morning*
to *Good evening*

That crow—
now be good
and stop crying

On a green summer night,
a horse of glass
neighs in the distance

ブラウス透けて薫風が見えそう

二歳の沈黙はマシュマロのかたち

朝曇おんなの身体ひらきやすくて

A cloudy morning—
a woman's body
opens easily

The silence
of a two-year-old—
the shape of marshmallows

Through her blouse
you can almost see
the summer breeze

青葉から離れず今日という光

この百合が咲かない見つめているのに

男とは紅薔薇にぎくしゃくと寄る

Men are those
who approach roses
awkwardly

This lily won't bloom—
even though
I'm staring at it

Unable to depart
the young leaves—
a light called *today*

雲雀鳴く空は甘いかしょっぱいか

入道雲天より大きくなりたいと

向日葵きいろ退屈はなにいろ

The sunflower's yellow—
what color
is boredom?

The thunderhead says
it wants to grow bigger
than the heavens

A skylark sings—
is the sky
salty or sweet?

雲の数ひとつに戻り夏つづく

川は海へ目も口もあけたまま

あと三つあれば楽しいさくらんぼ

It'd be more fun
if there were three more
fresh cherries

The river empties
into the sea—its eyes and
mouth wide open

The number of clouds
returns to one—
summer continues

君はいま枕よりパリより遠い

虹よ私はなぜここにいるのだろう

ひく波に剥がされてゆく貝の夢

Dreams of a clam
torn away
in the undertow

Hey, rainbow!
Tell me,
why am I here?

You are now
further than your pillow,
further than Paris

曼珠沙華なり赤ならば捨てるほど

うろこ雲結んで開いて失って

「夏は終る」木の股で小鬼がつぶやく

50

Summer's over
mutters a goblin
in the tree crotch

A mackerel sky—
expanding, opening,
and disappearing

A red spider lily—
it's so red
I want to throw it out

川知らず此処で凍ってしまうとは

階段はまだ眠るらし冬つまづく

きれいなど言うはずもなく冬鏡

It won't say things
like *you're pretty*—
the winter mirror

The stairs still seem
to be sleeping—
tripping in winter

The river here
doesn't know it will
become frozen

皿に皿かさねて春を待ちぼうけ

怒るより咲いてしまおうクロッカス

木の芽らに空がすやすや陽もすやすや

On the tree buds
the sky sleeps soundly,
the sun sleeps soundly

Let's just bloom
instead of getting angry—
the crocuses

Placing a plate
on a plate, waiting
in vain for spring

はるのかぜ丸も四角も三角も

青空とすこしの勇気梅ひらく

土わすれ私をわすれ蕗のとう

Forgetting the soil
and forgetting me—
the butterbur sprouts bloom

With a blue sky
and a little courage,
the plum bud opens

The spring wind
is a circle, a square
and a triangle

その人の隣りに椿は落ちたい

散るさくら目をつむるのも瞑らぬも

鴎に問わん海おおう天の来歴

Let's ask the seagulls
about the origin of the sky
that blankets the sea

Scattering cherry blossoms—
closing my eyes
and not closing my eyes

The camellia flower
wants to drop
next to that man

花菜畑ひかりが帰る道もいくらか

桜草ゆれてもゆれても風が痛い

あてど無き蒲公英絮が二十、百

Without any idea
the dandelion fuzz
becomes twenty, a hundred

Even as the primrose
trembles and trembles
the wind is still hurtful

In a field of mustard flowers
just a few ways
for the light to return home

くちびるの気ままを許す赤林檎

睡蓮の葉ですそよろと座りませ

桜しべもうすぐ土を好きになる

Cherry blossom stamens
soon learn
to like the earth

This is a swaying
water lily leaf—
won't you take a seat?

A red apple
allows the lips
to do what they like

向日葵に問いたし丸く生きる

「暑いってば」吹き方を忘れた風に

金魚玉の水若ければ三周め

Water in the goldfish bowl—
if it's fresh
the fish make a third lap

Hey, it's hot!
I said to the wind
that forgot how to blow

I want to ask the sunflower
about the art
of living simply

枯れたくない風がケヤキで大暴れ

A wind that doesn't want to die
goes on a rampage   .
against a zelkova

砂

Sand

赤は砂、白も砂、黒も砂にしかず

モロッコは風あそぶ国　星はあす見る

ひかりの上どかと光が座る夏

The light sits down
on the sunlight with a flop
in summertime

Morocco is a country where the wind plays

I'll look for the stars
tomorrow

Redness is sand,
whiteness, too, is sand,
and blackness is certainly sand

テーブルに蝶まどろめばスプーンも

オアシスはヤシ、鳥、小石やがて月

愛をさがす天使にも蝿にも羽を

Searching for love,
angels and flies
have wings attached

An oasis is palm trees,
birds and pebbles,
and before long, the moon

At the table
a butterfly dozes off,
a spoon, too

光には負けませんよと黒揚羽

どくだみのどこが私に似てるというの

ひまわりの空は遅れてやってくる

The sky over
the sunflower
is running late

Which part of
the fishwort
resembles me?

I won't be defeated
by the light
says the spangle butterfly

どの砂か砂漠にひとり消えたのは

蜂はジュースに戯れやがて溺れる

ドーナツの穴をくぐって夏つづく

Passing through
the hole of a donut,
summer continues

A bee plays in juice
and drowns
before too long

Which grain of sand
disappeared alone
into the desert?

砂の塔すなを信じて砂にそびえる

ひかりに飽きたお日様が沈みます

猫が目をほそめる夏は風になった

A cat narrows its eyes—
the summer
turned into wind

Tired of shining,
the honorable sun
begins to set

A tower of sand—
believe in the sand
rising up in the sand

モザイクに閉じ込められし兄王子

砂粒発つ千と二つめの夜へ

モロッコは饒舌ひかりも人も

Moroccans are loquacious—
the sunlight
and the people

A grain of sand departs
toward one thousand
and two nights

Trapped inside
a mosaic—
the elder prince

生きるべく砂粒はころぶ砂漠に

猫にはチーズほら穴には呪文

夜を掴むシェヘラザードの長き腕

Catching the evening,
the long arms
of Scheherazade

A piece of cheese
for the cat, an incantation
for the cave

To feel alive
a grain of sand
tumbles in the desert

玉葱には紐を旧市街（カスバ）に迷わぬよう

風の国に風をきらいなヤシが一本

マラケシュにアリババを待つ壺三つ

In Marrakesh,
three teapots
await Ali Baba

Within the kingdom of wind,
there's one palm tree
that hates the wind

Tie up the bag of onions
with string so we don't lose it
and ourselves in the Kasbah!

きみは歩く砂漠を金色にせんと

蹴られ流され固まり古ぶ砂漠

ここは雀にそこは蜘蛛にヤシの葉陰

This spot for a sparrow,
that spot for a spider,
under the leaves of a palm tree

Kicked, swept away,
and hardening—
the aging desert

You start walking,
trying to turn the desert
into gold

空は秋さてどの雲について行こう

虹すこしアリババの壺の油に

塔は立つ捨ててしまった夕日のために

The tower stands in
for a sunset
that's been discarded

A little rainbow
inside
Ali Baba's oil jars

The sky is autumn itself—
now,
let's follow a cloud!

あめんぼの後から水がのっしのっし

イタリアはおいしいですと蟻の列

天は地平にすわり永遠を考える

The sky sits
on the horizon,
reflecting on eternity

Italy is delicious
A row of ants
at work

In the wake of a water strider,
the water
lumbers on

背のびして二歳は星を覚えはじめる

ウィスキーに酔ったか氷溶けはじむ

熊蜂に玻璃はいよいよ硬くなる

Because of the bumblebee
the windowpane
hardens more and more

Are you drunk
from the whiskey?
The ice starts to melt

Stretching his back
a two-year-old begins
to remember a star

「ボンジョルノ」カーテンが菫に挨拶

物語は母と出会えりいつか風も

夏の音階ソとラのあいだ雲浮いて

Summer's musical scale:
between sol and la
a cloud floats past

In the story,
he met his mother—
one day the wind, too

Buongiorno—
the curtains
greet the violets

午後をべとべとにして羽虫は集う

月明かり屋根から枝へ窓へ眼へ

壁にハムにパルマは健やかなピンク

From the ham
to the house walls
Parma is a healthy pink

Under moonlight
from a rooftop
toward a branch, a window, an eye

The lice gather
stickily
in the afternoon

線路へことり列車まだ来ないよと

明日を探そう水なき川の橋を渡って

雀のおしゃべり「モナリザを見たかい」

Sparrows chatting—
"Did you see
the *Mona Lisa?*"

Let's search for tomorrow—
crossing the bridge
over a river without water

A small bird approaches
the tracks—hey,
the train hasn't come yet

フレスコ画から赤が消えマリアも消えた

パルマ産チーズが笑いつつ篭へ

右手はカンツォーネ左手は星空

In the right hand
a *canzone*—
in the left, a starry sky

Cheese from Parma
goes laughing
into the basket

From a fresco
the red has faded—
Mary's faded, too

イエスをしたう敷石は糞乗せたまま

木の葉ふる大地のつかれ癒すべく

広場で買う水には夕焼のおまけ

In the piazza
buying water with
a free sunset

Tree leaves fall
to heal
the earth's exhaustion

Yearning for Jesus,
the cobblestones
bearing horseshit

木の葉ちり風は散らずにわたくしへ

サフランはそっと受けとる雨と鐘の音

塔は思う空はいつまでいてくれるか

The tower thinks:
how long will
the sky remain?

The saffron receives quietly
the rain
and the sound of a bell

Tree leaves scattering—
the leftover wind
blowing toward me

初景色ひかりの音が聞こえそう

知っています菫が揺れることならば

あおいろを空に還して夏終る

Returning its blue
back to the sky
the summer ends

I know it—
if a violet
is shaking

Sights on the first day
of the new year—
sounds like the sound of light

靴音に色あらば冬空の青

川には水を春と出合うところまで

勝てば晴れ負けても晴れの独楽回し

If I win or lose,
it's a fine day—
spinning a top

Water in the river
to the point
it meets the spring

If the sound of footsteps
has a color,
it's the winter sky's blue

蹴ってしまおう小石ほどの寒さは

凍ててゆく星々なれば数えずに

吹きに吹く木枯しは何が欲しいの

Blow after blow—
what do you want,
winter wind?

Colder and colder—
no more counting
all those stars tonight

I reject it:
the cold
like a pebble—

くるぶしにワルツを纏い春の中へ

クロッカス萌えるとは少しはばたく

空よ君を失うわけにはいかぬ

Oh, sky!
I cannot
lose you

A crocus sprouts—
it flaps
just a little

Wrapping a waltz
around my ankle
I go into spring

鐘の音ぺこん大空に叱られた

獣の骨たぶんそこらに冬の骨も

雪ふれふれ今さら天に戻れねば

Snow falling and falling—
too late
to return to the sky

Bones from a beast—
there's also probably
a bone of winter

The sound of a bell
as if caving in—
scolded by the sky

寝て起きて塵とあそんで春を待つ

I sleep, get up,
and play with the dust—
waiting for spring

雲

Clouds

泥も少しわが額ほどの雪に

時々はちちははを呼び芽吹きおり

引き出しの中では歌うホッチキス

120

Inside a drawer
a stapler
singing away

Sometimes
I call out for my mother and father—
like a sprouting bud

A bit of mud
on a patch of snow
as big as my forehead

真っ白な雲にはあたたかな空を

さくら三日め散るのが怖くなっている

咲く痛み咲けぬ痛みも花のころ

Painful to bloom,
painful not to bloom
in this time of flowers

Third day of cherry blossoms—
I'm afraid
to see them scatter

A pure white cloud
and the warm sky
moving toward it

「もういいかい」釘の頭がまだ見える

波とあそぶ一人ぼっち岩ぼっち

たなごころ皺も一緒に春になろう

In the palm of the hand
even wrinkles
turn into spring together

Playing with the waves—
my loneliness
and a solitary rock

Ready or not!
I can still see
the head of a nail

赤を捨て黄を捨て夕やけは遊ぶ

「通りゃんせ」五月の空はドアいらぬ

雲ちょっとどいてブランコが行くよ

A cloud withdraws a bit
and this swing
starts to take off

Go on through!
The sky in May
doesn't need a door

Shedding its reds
and shedding its yellows
the sunset still plays

寒の文字けしても消してもまだ寒い

日をかしこみ風をかしこみ梅一花

靴ひもに春を告げんと蝶結び

My shoelaces
tied in a bow
herald the spring

In awe of the day,
in awe of the wind—
one plum flower

Even if I delete
a letter in *cold*
it's still cold

ちりぬるを桜も笑みも散りぬるを

グラスから空の生れて京は春

戸を閉めて鍵かけて冬終らせる

Closing a door
and locking it—
the winter ends

The sky's born
from glass—
Kyoto is springtime

The cherry blossoms
and all those smiles
will scatter eventually

ウサギ寝てカメ見えざれば影も寝る

舞う蝶に背骨はどうしても曲る

黄のちゃらんぽらんも菜の花の盛り

The carelessness of yellow—
mustard flowers
in full bloom

No matter what
I twist my back
to see the dancing butterflies

The rabbit sleeps
and its shadow follows,
unaware of the tortoise

出航の夜ぞ星々を召還せよ

部屋おぼろ私がここにいるというのに

黄昏をはぐくむ真水、爪、白髪

134

Rearing the dusk:
fresh water, fingernails,
and my gray hair

The room seems dim
even though
I'm sitting here

The night of your departure—
summon back
the stars and planets

面会は昼から夕日が揺れるまで

陽は昇るコップの中の水平線にも

そのブナの緑を濃くするのは君だ

It is you
who darkens the green
of that beech tree

The sun rises
over the water's horizon
inside a cup

The hospital visit lasts
from the afternoon
until the sunset trembles

石榴割ってその実の多きこと畏^{おそ}る

スリッパに廊下は痛いほど広し

ひまわりの茎ものぼって君の元へ

石榴割ってその実の多きこと畏る

スリッパに廊下は痛いほど広し

ひまわりの茎ものぼって君の元へ

The sunflower stems
and me
climbing up toward you

This corridor is so large
it hurts
my slippers

Breaking open a pomegranate,
I'm awed
by its many seeds

泣くまじく天井はひたすら硬い

指は知る夏の日ざしのこわばるを

風動くな夫の手術もうすぐ終る

Wind, don't move—
my husband's operation
will end soon

My finger can tell:
the summer sunlight
is hardening

I'm not going to cry—
like that ceiling
remaining so firm

うつぶせの辛さ蛇にもわかるかい

夫よ眠れ星が生れる窓のとなりに

針一本に腕をあずけて透きとおる

Leaving one needle
in the arm,
now it's see-through

Sleep, my husband,
next to the window
with a newborn star in it

The pain of lying
on one's face—
does a snake know it?

光りさす手すりづたいに癒えるべし

病院が日傘の下に遠く小さく

青田波やさしい神を呼ぶように

Rolling waves of rice—
like calling
to a tender god

A hospital
under an umbrella:
far and small

Sunlight streaming
along a handrail—
you must be cured

水の旅は口から喉へはらわたへ

朝の点滴は蓮ひらく速さで

「クルックー」ノアが放ちし鳩が窓辺に

Coo, coo—
the dove Noah released
at the window

In the morning,
an intravenous drip with the speed
of a lotus opening

The journey of water
from the mouth to the throat
to the bowels

妻はわたし薔薇に休んで爪噛んで

閉めないで天使も通るドアなれば

星は夜に夫は管につながれる

Like stars to the night,
my husband
tied to tubes

Don't close that door—
an angel
may pass through

I'm the wife—
stopping to smell roses,
chewing on my nails

仮初の仮の字として涼しけれ

草いきれ道なきことを楽しめと

ベンチには蟻一匹と涙ひとつぶ

Sitting on a bench
with one ant
and a single tear

The strong smell of grass—
enjoying not having
a path ahead

As refreshing
as the "trans"
in transience—

かき氷羽ばたきながら溶けもする

白雲の崩れやすさも癒えるため

夫留守の水にナイフが溺れそう

My husband absent—
in the dishwater
a knife seems to be drowning

To be cured
with the ease of clouds
breaking

Shaved ice
even in flight
also melts

四人が座る病室はどこも明るい

夫が描くみどりの木々とその匂い

歩けあるけ月に遅れをとろうとも

154

Moon, keep walking
and walking,
even if you fall behind

My husband draws—
green trees
and their smell

Four family members sitting
in the hospital room—
everywhere is sunlit

靴先に日を止まらせて極月へ

父の空ゆっくり家族の空になる

枕のくぼみに君の夢ふたたび

Into the hollow
of your pillow—
the dream again

A father's sky
slowly becomes
his family's sky

Let the day end
at the point of your shoes
facing December

うり坊うろうろ春落ちてないかな

はるかなる風も結んで注連飾り

これは寂しさの重さか手の木の葉

Is this the weight
of loneliness?
A tree leaf in my hand

A far-off wind's
also tied to them—
sacred ropes at a shrine

A wild boar's offspring
walking aimlessly—
has spring not arrived yet?

風澄みぬ私がわたしに会えるよう

うろこ雲ひらくのが好き消えるのも

春風が笑顔を配達しています

A spring breeze
delivering
a smiling face

The mackerel sky
likes opening
and disappearing

The wind is so clear
it seems
I can meet myself

白鳥待つ水面に空が眩しすぎる

天高し指に言っても仕方ないけど

妹から姉へコスモスが揺れる

From the younger sister
to the older sister—
the field of cosmos flowers sways

The sky's so vast—
even if I tell my finger to join it
there's nothing it can do

The water's surface
waiting for a swan—
the sky's too radiant

冬うらら風もベンチにお座りよ

月光をさやさや連れて年越さん

水酸っぱし枯れながら薔薇が吸うとき

Sour water—
a dying rose
soaks it up

Moonlight
rustling from the old year
into the new one

A clear winter's day—
wind, have a seat
with me on this bench

北風はあのブナの樹に帰りたい

雪は降る窓辺が飽きてしまっても

夕焼の代わりに枯れて芒原

Instead of a sunset,
the pampas grass
withers and dies

Snow keeps falling—
even the window's
getting tired of it

The north wind
wants to return
to that beech tree

古い靴音をさがしに石畳

白薔薇に枯れてと頼んだのは私

丘が招く春のうたげは自転車で

Invited by the hills
to a spring banquet,
going by bicycle

It was me
who asked the white rose
to wither

Looking for the sound
of old footsteps
on the cobblestones

雪は地を黙は机を埋めつくす

始まりも終りもなくて玉こんにゃく

本当に吹きたいですかと木枯しに

170

Does it really
want to blow—
the winter wind?

Neither a beginning
nor an ending—
a ball of *konnyaku* jelly

Snow on the ground,
silence piling up
around the desk

空に棲むひかりの部屋はたぶん楕円

梅ひらく胸も肩も無防備なれば

草の芽へ風は歩いてくるらしい

To grass sprouts
the wind seems
to come walking

A plum flower opens—
my chest and shoulders
are defenseless, too

That room of light
dwelling in the sky
is probably oval

狭き門いよいよ狭く花ふぶく

鯨は潮吹く春よりも高くたかく

デージーの隣りで豚の尻尾くるん

A daisy blooms
next to the curling tail
of a little pig

The whale spouts
higher and higher
than spring

The narrow gate
narrows and narrows
in a storm of cherry blossoms

血も爪もたぶん桜には必要

ロバの耳王様の耳など知らぬ

芝に下ろそうバッグも母という文字も

Sitting on the grass—
tired of my bag
and motherhood

A donkey's ears—
they don't know about
the King's ears and such

Blood and nails
are probably necessary
for a cherry tree

春惜しむ口紅にくち与えつつ

花びらを海に届けて暮れている

白木蓮ふたりで咲いて一人ふるえる

178

The white magnolia—
two people blooming,
one person shaking

Sending petals
into the sea
and the sun setting

Lamenting the end of spring
as I give my mouth
some lipstick

彦星を待たせて織姫は歌う

土と呼ぶな踏まれることに飽きたのだ

ふと飛んで紋白蝶は飛びつづける

Taking off suddenly,
the small white butterfly
keeps flying away

Don't call me *soil*—
I'm tired of being
trampled upon

Keeping Altair
waiting
Vega sings

星に生れて仰がれる淋しさよ

叱られた水かも井戸の底にいる

草抜くとまず掴むその首のあたり

To pull up grass
first I grab
around the neck

The water at the bottom
of the well has
probably been scolded

Born as a star
whom do you look up to?
Such loneliness

その塀の罅をあらわに初明り

父から子へ風から風へ星の神話

明日もひまわり茎の汚れを風で拭いて

Tomorrow's a sunflower, too—
dirt on the stem
blown away by the wind

From a father to a child,
from wind to wind—
the mythology of stars

A crack in that wall
revealed
at first light

天にある去年や如何にと背伸びする

初恋をほったらかしにして嚔

枯れてあげる風がもっと遊べるように

A tree dies so the
wind can rise
and play more

Neglecting
my first love,
I sneeze

Last year in the sky:
I stretch myself
to see how it's doing

蛇口からいもうとの水あねの水

こちらへこちらへ羽衣が空を招く

ト音記号くるくる春の港まで

The treble clef curves
round and round
as far as the spring harbor

This way, this way!
The feathered robe
invites the sky along

From a faucet:
the younger sister's water,
the older sister's water

黙祷のあとはフォークの出番です

草揺れる草にも来世あるごとく

トマトに塩ふって昨日においとまを

Sprinkling salt on a tomato,
I say good-bye
to yesterday

The grass sways
as if grass
had an afterlife

After a silent prayer
it's the time
for forks

枝よりも幹を信じて木の葉散る

冬始まる押入れに風閉じこめて

午後二時五分バナナを剥けば六分に

2:05 PM—
if I peel this banana
it's 2:06 PM

It begins in winter:
shutting the wind
inside a closet

More than the branches,
they trust the trunk:
the scattering leaves

春だ春だ蛇口から水にぎやかに

極月の階を下りつつ腕さまよう

シチューには人参、じゃがいも、「ただいま」を

Inside a stew:
carrots, potatoes,
I'm home!

While going down
stairs in December,
my arm wanders

It's spring, it's spring!
Water runs cheerfully
from the faucet

星の茶会にオリオンは今宵も遅刻

枯れるのはその位にしてわが欅

子を生みしことも真青にわたしの空

Thinking back on mothering,
I gaze up
at an entirely blue sky

Stop withering
right there—
my zelkova tree

Orion's late again
for the stars' tea party
this evening

もっと青くなれると大空から便り

芽吹かざる肘をさそって春の野へ

幹に手を添えても梢はまだ寒い

Even if I put my hand on the tree trunk
the tips of its branches
remain cold

Tempting the branch's elbow
that doesn't bud—
the spring fields

I can turn pure blue—
tidings
from the sky

雲へ拍手じょうずに春を呼べました

風をあやつるアメノウズメの臍なりき

やがて咲くさくらのために遠回り

Soon enough
I make a detour
for the blooming cherry tree

The goddess of the dawn
plays the wind
with her belly button

Applause for a cloud—
you did such a fine job
of calling for spring

風

Wind

赤い風船母に逢えたら戻っておいで

泣き顔は見せたくないと膝小僧

花びらが橋を渡りに行くところ

A flower petal
on its way
to cross a bridge

Kneecaps
that don't want to show
their tearful faces

Red balloon—
come back if you can meet
your mother

身のほどを知れよと川を氷らせる

春の字の消去は親指にまかせた

ノートから飛び立ちキャベツ畑にいる

It flew off
from my notebook
into the cabbage patch

I let my thumb
delete
the word *spring*

Someone said
Know your place
and froze the river

春を探しにキリンの首の途中から

山を越すスミレの風になりたくて

水底は水を抱きしめ如月へ

The river bottom
hugs the water
into February

I want to be the wind
blowing violets
over the mountains

Searching for spring
half way up
a giraffe's neck

ヒヤシンス急行はいつも素通り

妻の座は猫のあくびの真正面

チューリップ今からここから私の時間

Tulips—
from now on
it's my time

The wife's seat:
right in front
of the cat's yawning

The hyacinths—
an express train is
always passing through

ポケットの春は紙くずとともに

壺の菜の花こんな黄色でいいかしら

遠い雲二月十日と書き終えて

212

A faraway cloud—
finished writing
on February 10th

Mustard flowers
in the vase:
does this yellow look good?

Spring in the pocket
along with
scraps of paper

風呂の湯の汚れっぷりも花のころ

木馬だって走れる暖かくなれば

わかるのは誰の椿も落ちること

All I know
is that anyone's camellia flowers
will drop

Even a wooden horse
would run
if it gets warm enough

Hot water in the bath
getting nicely dirty—
cherry blossom season.

大なべを空っぽにして春はゆく

柄杓もて春を回そうこおろこおろ

カーテンに隠れて窓が老いるとは

216

That window
grows old
behind the curtain

Let's churn spring
with a long ladle—
kōro-kōro

Emptying
a giant pot—
spring has passed

引き出しのおさない恋文へ星を

五ページから十ページまで麦麦麦

向日葵をわたしの空の入口に

Sunflowers
at the entrance
of my sky

From page five
to page ten
wheat wheat wheat

A star moves
toward my childish love letters
inside a drawer

列に入ろう一匹の蟻なれば

肋骨はならんで春を見送った

手のひらに爪を咲かせる夏は来ぬ

The summer has come
to my fingernails
blooming in my palms

My ribs lined up
and said farewell
to spring

Join the line
if you're
a single ant

マスクしていても西から雷が

黄バラ紅バラうち重なって無防備に

鼠は夢で地平線を少しかじった

In his dream
the mouse nibbled a bit
on the horizon

Yellow and red roses
lying on each other
defenselessly

Even wearing a mask—
thunder
from the west

風に書きし死の字が風から離れない

朕は靴なりなぜ砂が混じるか

姫は眠りそのスカートもゆっくり眠った

The princess slept
and her skirt seemed
to sleep well, too.

I am a noble shoe—
so why does sand
always get inside me?

The character for *death*
I write in the wind
is not separate from the wind

直線はコバルトブルーと決めて夏

むしろ空深く潜ろう入道雲

捨てられるバケツの音はドンガラン

The sound of a bucket
being thrown away:
don-ga-ran

A thunderhead
diving
into the deep end of the sky

The horizon fixed
as cobalt blue—
in the summertime

草いきれ草のことなど忘れました

本当は二つかも　夏の太陽

空はまだ大丈夫よと梅太る

The sky's still alright
says the plum
growing fat

Actually it could be two things

A summer sun

Such a strong smell
of summer grass—
the grass has forgotten itself

風も老いも隠してひまわりの迷路

鋏は知るや剪られゆく薔薇の痛み

「お下げしますね」ちり取りが蝉殻に

I shall remove you
says the dustpan
to the cicada husks

The scissors know
the rose's pain
as soon as they prune

The wind and old age
hidden by a maze
made of sunflowers

尖ること枝に許してケヤキ涼し

「さようなら」蟻は触角で受けとる

走れトカゲ背中の瑠璃を守るべく

Run, lizard,
protect the lapis lazuli jewel
on your back

Sayonara—
the ant understands
with its antennae

Pardon the sharpness
of its branches—
the refreshing zelkova tree

春色のリボンは明日入荷します

雲よりも肘をとおくに独楽まわし

雲が消えその白色も消える夏

A cloud disappears—
its white color, too,
disappears in summer

Farther than a cloud—
throwing my elbow into the distance
while spinning a top

Ribbons
with a touch of spring
will be in stock tomorrow

草の絮きみが発つときは私も

紅(くれない)のほどけやすくて吾亦紅

芒原うふふと空がもぐり込む

Saying *hee-hee*
the sky slips into
the pampas grass

The burnet's
deep red
easily comes undone

When the tufts
of grass depart,
so, too, will I

水に耳あらば塞げよ氷るとき

風も波もガラスの硬さアンドロメダ姫に

「冬が来るのね」橋桁は川に尋ねる

"Winter's come, hasn't it?"
the bridge girder
inquired of the river

For Princess Andromeda
the wind and waves
have the hardness of glass

If the water has ears
cover them up
when it freezes!

粉雪ちらちらレシートひらひら

サンタクロース急げば星もいそぐ

オリオンの下でスサノオは泣いた

The god Susanoo
cried
under Orion

If Santa Claus
hurries, the stars
will hurry too

Flurries of
powdered snow,
a receipt fluttering

信じたし初夢の青は鳥だったと

年越すと階段に手すりを探す

猛吹雪おみくじは吉だったけど

In the middle of a snowstorm—
my fortune slip from the shrine
was supposed to be good luck

Passing into the new year—
I look for a handrail
on the staircase

I want to believe the blue
I saw in my first dream
of the new year was a bird

お釈迦さまは立ち去り蜘蛛の糸ぶらん

そっと重ねる我より長く生きる皿

たいまつを掲げよ春が見えるはず

Raise your torchlight!
It's supposed
to reveal spring

Stacked gently
the plates
will outlive me

The Lord Buddha walks away—
a spider's thread
dangles in the air

山眠る石のくぼみに風残し

君とまだ出会わぬ頃へ水澄みぬ

こころもちワインは揺れて秋を知る

From my pinky
now to my middle finger—
first sunrise of the new year

First morning of the new year—
to complete the scene
let's add a pinch of salt

Notes

February, The Month
According to Japan's lunar calendar, the characters for the second month are written as 如月 *kisaragi*, which shares the same pronunciation of the phrase 衣更着 *kisaragi*, literally, "wearing extra clothes."

The Kusanagi sword
The Kusanagi sword, literally "grass cutter," is a legendary weapon so named because it was said to have aided a great warrior's escape from a field of tall grass set ablaze by his enemies. The sword allowed him to cut down the grasses and control the wind, sending the fire back in his opponent's direction. As part of the three Imperial Regalia of Japan, it is supposedly in the possession of the Imperial Family of Japan, but cannot be displayed due to its divine status.

The moss phlox–
Moss phlox are pink flowers that bloom close to the ground in late spring, often carpeting entire fields. Their resemblance to cherry blossoms is considered a sign of cheerfulness. Due to their growing patterns, they are also associated with cooperation.

A mackerel sky–
A sky with cirrocumulus clouds is known as a "mackerel sky" in Japan and represents autumn.

A red spider lily—
The red spider lily is a poisonous flower traditionally grown near graves to deter pests. It is known as the flower of the dead and is thought to absorb the blood of corpses to gain its scarlet color.

Let's just bloom
The crocus is one of Japan's earliest flowers to bloom in the spring. Its bright color gives it connotations of high expectations and happiness.

Forgetting the soil
Due to their natural growing season, wild butterbur sprouts are considered heralds of spring.

The camellia flower
In bloom, the camellia represents various virtues in Japan. However, a falling camellia flower is associated with a decapitated head, because the flower falls to the ground intact instead of shedding its petals. Consequently, camellias are not supposed to be given as a gift to anyone who is hospitalized or ill.

Even as the primrose
Representing late spring, the primrose symbolizes desire and enduring love. It is noted for its resemblance to cherry blossoms.

In a field of mustard flowers
Mustard flowers or canola flowers are prolific wildflowers in Japan, and evoke gaiety and brightness. They grow in vivid yellow fields during the late spring.

Which part of
Fishwort is a common weed in Japan and connotes summer.

From the younger sister
Cosmos flowers represent mid-autumn. Depending on the color of the flower, they can symbolize harmony, humility, or a youthful innocence.

Neither a beginning
Konnyaku is a jelly-like food made from konjac, a tuber said to have medicinal qualities.

A donkey's ears—
This haiku refers to a widespread fable about a king who had the ears of a donkey and tried to keep it a secret.

Keeping Altair
Vega can see Altair only one night a year, when their constellations pass each other.

This way, this way!
The feathered robe, or *hagoromo*, is a garment worn by celestial maidens in Japanese folktales. It gives them the ability to fly and allows them to return to their home in the heavens.

Stop withering
The Japanese zelkova is a tree with mythological and religious significance, appearing in many legends, especially as something that can bring about a curse if destroyed. The trees are often planted

near shrines as symbols of protection. A withering Japanese zelkova represents winter.

The goddess of the dawn
Ame-no-Uzume, the Japanese goddess of the dawn, is known for her sensuality and divine dancing.

The hyacinths—
The hyacinth was introduced to Japan at the end of the Tokugawa period. It signals early spring.

Let's churn spring
The onomatopoetic term *kōro-kōro* describes churning seawater that's beginning to congeal. The poem evokes the Shintō deities (and siblings) Izanagi and Izanami, who churned the primordial waters with a heavenly jeweled spear. According to Japanese mythology, drops of brine from the spear coagulated and formed Onogoro Island, the first island of Japan. The siblings consummated their marriage on Onogoro and then made the rest of Japan's islands.

The god Susanoo
The younger brother of the sun goddess Amaterasu, Susanoo is the Japanese god of violent storms. Orion is a giant huntsman from Greek mythology.

I want to believe the blue
In Japan, it is believed that the first dream of the new year, *hatsuyume*, can predict your fortunes for the year. The most auspicious visions are of Mount Fuji, hawks, and eggplants, in that order.

The Lord Buddha walks away—
In Ryūnosuke Akutagawa's short story "The Spider's Thread," the Lord Buddha lowers a spider thread down to a man as a way to escape from hell. The man manages to climb partly upwards, but the thread snaps under the weight of his ego.

Acknowledgments

Grateful acknowledgment is made to the publications in which these poems and translations were first published: *Ginyu, Haiku Shiki, Haiku World, Horizon: The Haiku Anthology* (India), *Saitama Shinbun, Two Lines* (USA), and *Yomiuri Shinbun*.

About the author

Sayumi Kamakura is the author of numerous poetry collections, including *Moisture*, *Cross in the Water*, *From the Skylight*, *La La La Goes the Sea*, and *The Collected Haiku of Sayumi Kamakura*. Her work has appeared in dozens of anthologies in Japan and overseas, and she is the only haiku poet featured in *Japanese Women Poets: An Anthology* edited by Hiroaki Sato. She has received the Oki Sango Prize, Modern Haiku Association Prize, and the Azsacra International Poetry Award. In 1998, she established the haiku magazine *Ginyu* with Ban'ya Natsuishi, and continues to serve as its coeditor.

About the translator

James Shea is the author of three poetry collections, *Last Day of My Face*, *The Lost Novel*, and *Star in the Eye*. He is the coeditor of *The Routledge Global Haiku Reader* and cotranslator of *Moving a Stone: Selected Poems of Yam Gong*. A recipient of grants from the Fulbright U.S. Scholar Program, National Endowment for the Arts, and Vermont Arts Council, he lives in Hong Kong.